Effortless Breaking Free Principles: Overcoming Financial Anxiety and achieving maximum success in life and business.

By

Banks Peterson

Introduction:	8
Chapter 1: Understanding Financial Anxiety	11
Chapter 2: Changing Your Money Mindset	22
Chapter 3: Developing Financial Literacy and Skills	32
Chapter 4: Setting Realistic Goals and Taking Action	44
Chapter 5 : Seeking Support and Building Resilience	54

All rights reserved. No part of this publication may be reproduced, distributed, or transmitted in any form or by any means, including Photocopying, Recording, or other electronic or mechanical methods, without the prior written permission of the publisher, except in the case of brief quotations embodied in critical reviews and certain other noncommercial uses permitted by copyright Law.

Copyright © Banks Peterson (2024)

Introduction:

Financial anxiety is a common and often debilitating experience that many men face in today's world. Whether it stems from mounting debt, job insecurity, or the pressure to provide for one's family, the burden of financial stress can take a significant toll on mental and emotional well-being. Here, we will explore the root causes of financial anxiety in men, examine its impact on mental health, and provide practical strategies for overcoming it.

Chapter 1: Understanding Financial Anxiety

Financial anxiety is more than just a concern about money—it is a pervasive sense of worry and fear that can consume every aspect of a man's life. Financial anxiety can manifest in a variety of ways, from constant worry and sleep disturbances to physical symptoms such as headaches or stomachaches. Financial anxiety in men can be influenced by various factors, including:

1. Economic Uncertainty: Economic instability, job insecurity, or fluctuating income can contribute to feelings of financial insecurity and anxiety. Men may feel pressure to provide for their families or maintain a certain standard of living, leading to heightened stress about financial stability.

2. Social Comparisons: Men may compare themselves to others in terms of income,

wealth, or material possessions, leading to feelings of inadequacy or failure if they perceive themselves as falling short. Social media and societal expectations can exacerbate these comparisons, fueling financial anxiety.

3. Family Responsibilities: The responsibility of providing for a family, including spouse, children, or aging parents, can amplify financial stress. Men may feel pressure to meet financial

obligations and ensure the well-being of their loved ones, leading to heightened anxiety about finances.

4. Debt and Financial Obligations: Accumulated debt, such as student loans, credit card debt, or mortgage payments, can contribute to financial anxiety in men. Concerns about repaying debt, interest rates, and financial obligations can weigh heavily on their minds, impacting overall well-being.

5. Career Pressures: Expectations to advance in one's career, achieve financial success, or meet societal standards of success can contribute to stress and anxiety. Men may feel pressured to excel in their professions, leading to heightened anxiety about job performance, promotions, or earning potential.

6. Lack of Financial Literacy: Limited knowledge about personal finance,

budgeting, investing, or retirement planning can exacerbate financial anxiety. Men may feel overwhelmed or ill-equipped to manage their finances effectively, leading to heightened stress about financial matters.

7. Relationship Dynamics: Financial disagreements or conflicts within relationships, such as disagreements about spending habits, financial priorities, or unequal financial contributions, can

contribute to stress and anxiety. Men may feel pressure to navigate these issues while maintaining harmony in their relationships.

8. Cultural and Societal Expectations: Cultural norms and societal expectations regarding masculinity, success, and financial independence can influence men's perceptions of themselves and their financial situations. Pressure to conform to

these expectations can contribute to heightened anxiety about finances.

Overall, financial anxiety in men can stem from a combination of economic, social, psychological, and relational factors. Addressing these underlying factors and seeking support from trusted individuals or professionals can help men manage and alleviate financial anxiety.

Chapter 2: Changing Your Money Mindset

Our beliefs and attitudes about money play a significant role in shaping our financial behaviors and outcomes. A money mindset that leads to financial anxiety can be characterized by various beliefs, attitudes, and behaviors that contribute to heightened stress and worry about money.

Some common money mindsets that may lead to financial anxiety include:

1. Scarcity Mindset: Believing that there is never enough money to meet one's needs or desires can lead to constant worry and fear about financial security. Individuals with a scarcity mindset may focus on what they lack rather than what they have, leading to feelings of deprivation and anxiety.

2. Fear of Failure: A fear of failure or loss can cause individuals to avoid taking financial risks or making necessary changes to improve their financial situation. This fear can lead to paralysis, preventing individuals from making proactive decisions to address financial challenges and pursue opportunities for growth.

3. Perfectionism: Striving for perfection in financial matters can lead to unrealistic

expectations and constant dissatisfaction with one's financial situation. Perfectionists may feel overwhelmed by the pressure to achieve financial success, leading to anxiety and stress about meeting impossibly high standards.

4. Avoidance Behavior: Avoiding financial tasks such as budgeting, saving, or investing can exacerbate financial anxiety. Individuals who avoid confronting their financial situation may feel overwhelmed

by uncertainty and lack of control, leading to increased stress and worry.

5. Comparison Trap: Constantly comparing oneself to others in terms of financial success, possessions, or lifestyle can fuel feelings of inadequacy and insecurity. This comparison trap can lead to a sense of never measuring up, causing anxiety and dissatisfaction with one's financial situation.

6. Money as a Measure of Self-Worth: Linking one's self-worth to financial success or material possessions can lead to heightened anxiety and stress. Individuals who equate their value as individuals with their financial status may feel constant pressure to prove themselves, leading to anxiety about maintaining or improving their financial position.

7. Negative Beliefs About Money: Holding negative beliefs about money,

such as "money is the root of all evil" or "I don't deserve to be wealthy," can contribute to feelings of guilt, shame, or unworthiness about financial success. These beliefs can undermine confidence and create barriers to building wealth, leading to financial anxiety.

8. Lack of Financial Literacy: A lack of knowledge or understanding about personal finance can contribute to feelings of insecurity and anxiety about money.

Individuals who feel ill-equipped to manage their finances may avoid making financial decisions or seek guidance, leading to increased stress and worry.

Addressing and challenging these negative money mindsets through awareness, education, and practical strategies can help individuals cultivate a healthier relationship with money and alleviate financial anxiety. Through self-reflection and mindset shifts, men can begin to adopt healthier attitudes towards money and cultivate a sense of abundance and empowerment.

Chapter 3: Developing Financial Literacy and Skills

One of the most effective ways to combat financial anxiety is by arming oneself with knowledge and skills to manage money effectively. By taking control of their financial future and building a solid financial foundation, men can gain confidence and peace of mind in their ability to navigate financial challenges.

Financial literacy and skills are essential for managing money effectively and making informed financial decisions. Here are some key aspects of financial literacy and skills:

1. Budgeting: Budgeting involves creating a plan for how to allocate income towards expenses, savings, and investments. Understanding how to create and stick to a budget helps individuals prioritize

spending, track their financial goals, and manage cash flow effectively.

2. Saving and Investing: Saving involves setting aside money for short-term and long-term goals, such as emergencies, retirement, or major purchases. Investing involves putting money into assets such as stocks, bonds, or real estate with the expectation of generating returns over time. Understanding the principles of saving and investing helps individuals

build wealth and achieve their financial objectives.

3. Debt Management: Debt management involves understanding different types of debt, such as credit card debt, student loans, or mortgages, and developing strategies to manage and repay debt responsibly. This includes understanding interest rates, repayment terms, and the impact of debt on overall financial health.

4. Financial Planning: Financial planning involves setting financial goals, creating a roadmap to achieve those goals, and regularly reviewing and adjusting the plan as needed. This may include retirement planning, education planning, estate planning, and risk management strategies such as insurance.

5. Understanding Financial Products: Financial literacy includes knowledge of various financial products and services,

such as checking and savings accounts, credit cards, loans, insurance, and investment products. Understanding the features, costs, and risks associated with these products helps individuals make informed choices that align with their financial goals and values.

6. Tax Planning: Tax planning involves understanding the tax implications of financial decisions and taking steps to minimize tax liabilities legally. This

includes understanding tax deductions, credits, and strategies for tax-efficient investing and retirement planning.

7. Consumer Rights and Responsibilities: Financial literacy also encompasses knowledge of consumer rights and responsibilities when engaging in financial transactions. This includes understanding consumer protection laws, rights regarding financial products and services, and how to dispute errors or fraudulent charges.

8. Behavioral Finance: Behavioral finance explores how psychological biases and emotions influence financial decision-making. Understanding common behavioral biases, such as loss aversion or overconfidence, helps individuals make more rational and effective financial choices.

Developing financial literacy and skills is an ongoing process that requires education, practice, and continuous learning. By enhancing financial literacy and skills, individuals can take control of their financial futures, build wealth, and achieve their financial goals.

Chapter 4: Setting Realistic Goals and Taking Action

Overcoming financial anxiety requires setting realistic goals and taking consistent action towards achieving them. Setting realistic goals and taking action are essential steps for achieving success in any area of life, including personal finance.

Here's how to set realistic financial goals and take action to achieve them:

1. Assess Your Current Financial Situation: Start by evaluating your current financial status, including income, expenses, assets, debts, and savings. Understanding where you stand financially will help you set realistic goals that are achievable within your means.

2. Define Your Financial Goals: Identify short-term, medium-term, and long-term financial goals that align with your values and priorities. Short-term goals may include building an emergency fund or paying off credit card debt, while long-term goals may include saving for retirement or buying a home.

3. Make Your Goals Specific, Measurable, Achievable, Relevant, and Time-Bound (SMART): Ensure that your goals are

specific, measurable, achievable, relevant, and time-bound. For example, instead of saying "I want to save money," set a goal such as "I want to save $5,000 for a down payment on a house within the next two years."

4. Break Down Your Goals into Actionable Steps: Break down each goal into smaller, actionable steps that you can take to move closer to achieving them. For example, if your goal is to pay off credit

card debt, your action steps may include creating a budget, reducing discretionary spending, and increasing your debt payments.

5. Make a Spending plan: Foster a financial plan that mirrors your pay, costs, and monetary objectives. Distribute your pay towards fundamental costs, reserve funds, obligation installments, and optional spending.

6. Prioritize Your Goals: Determine which goals are most important to you and prioritize them accordingly. Focus your time, energy, and resources on achieving your top priorities, and consider delaying less critical goals if necessary.

7. Take Consistent Action: Take consistent action towards your financial goals by implementing the steps outlined in your action plan. Make a commitment to stick to your budget, track your progress

regularly, and make adjustments as needed to stay on course.

8. Stay Motivated and Persistent: Stay motivated and persistent, even when faced with obstacles or setbacks. Celebrate your successes along the way and use any setbacks as learning opportunities to adjust your approach and keep moving forward.

9. Seek Support and Accountability: Consider enlisting the support of family

members, friends, or a financial advisor to help you stay accountable and motivated towards achieving your goals. Share your progress with others and celebrate your achievements together.

By setting realistic financial goals and taking consistent action towards achieving them, you can take control of your finances and build a brighter financial future for yourself and your family.

Chapter 5 : Seeking Support and Building Resilience

No man is an island, and overcoming financial anxiety often requires seeking support from trusted friends, family members, or financial professionals. Seeking support and building resilience are crucial strategies for navigating challenges and overcoming obstacles in life, including financial setbacks. Here's how to seek support and cultivate resilience in the face of financial difficulties:

1. Reach Out to Trusted Individuals: Seek support from family members, friends, or mentors who can offer guidance, encouragement, and practical assistance during difficult times. Sharing your concerns and seeking advice from trusted individuals can provide emotional support and perspective on your situation.

2. Join Support Groups: Consider joining support groups or online communities where you can connect with others who are facing similar financial challenges. Participating in support groups can provide a sense of belonging, empathy, and shared experiences, as well as access to valuable resources and coping strategies.

3. Consult Financial Professionals: Seek guidance from financial professionals,

such as financial advisors, credit counselors, or debt management experts, who can offer personalized advice and assistance tailored to your specific financial situation. Working with a professional can help you develop a plan to address your financial challenges and achieve your goals.

4. Utilize Community Resources: Explore community resources and support services available in your area, such as financial

literacy workshops, job training programs, or assistance programs for low-income individuals and families. These resources can provide valuable education, assistance, and access to financial tools and services.

5. Practice Self-Care: Take care of your physical, emotional, and mental well-being by prioritizing self-care activities such as exercise, healthy eating, adequate sleep, and stress-reducing practices like mindfulness or meditation.

Taking care of yourself can help you cope with stress, maintain resilience, and stay focused on your goals.

6. Develop Coping Strategies: Identify and develop coping strategies that help you manage stress and maintain a positive outlook despite financial challenges. This may include practicing gratitude, maintaining a sense of humor, engaging in hobbies or activities that bring you joy, or

seeking professional counseling or therapy if needed.

7. Build Financial Resilience: Cultivate financial resilience by diversifying your income sources, building an emergency fund, reducing debt, and developing strong financial habits and skills. Building resilience can help you weather financial storms, bounce back from setbacks, and adapt to changing circumstances more effectively.

8. Stay Positive and Flexible: Maintain a positive attitude and remain flexible in your approach to overcoming financial challenges. Focus on solutions rather than dwelling on problems, and be open to adjusting your plans and strategies as needed to navigate changing circumstances.

By seeking support from others, practicing self-care, and cultivating resilience, you can effectively cope with financial difficulties, bounce back from setbacks, and ultimately build a stronger and more secure financial future for yourself and your family.

Conclusion:

Financial anxiety is a formidable foe, but it is not insurmountable. By understanding the root causes of financial anxiety, recognizing the signs and symptoms, and taking proactive steps towards financial empowerment, men can break free from the shackles of financial stress and reclaim control over their lives. With determination, resilience, and support, every man has the power to overcome financial anxiety and build a brighter, more secure future for himself and his loved ones.